NATIONAL
GEOGRAPHIC

Caring for Earth

Solomon Gordon

Earth is our home.
We need to take care of it.

How can we care for Earth?

We can plant trees.
Trees make fresh air for us to breathe.

We can pick up trash.
Trash pollutes the land.

We can recycle.
Soft drink cans, glass, and newspapers
can all be used again.

We can ride bikes instead of using a car.
Fumes from cars make the air dirty.

Everyone can help look after Earth.
What will you do to help?